Port Glasgow
Then & Now
Bill Clark

The town's Coat-of-Arms was granted on 14th November 1929. The motto reads, "Ter et Quater Anno Revisens Aequor Atlanticum Impune", which may be translated as: "Three and four times per year crossing the Atlantic with impunity".

Text © Bill Clark, 2023.
First published in the United Kingdom, 2023,
by Stenlake Publishing Ltd.,
54-58 Mill Square,
Catrine, Ayrshire,
KA5 6RD

Telephone: 01290 551122
www.stenlake.co.uk

ISBN 9781840339567

The publishers regret that they cannot supply copies of any pictures featured in this book.

Acknowledgements

Thanks to Tommy Rodger, who found a number of the *Then* images and helped to locate several of the original viewpoints.

Photographs on pages 14, 26, 28, 32 and 34 are reproduced with the permission of the McLean Museum in Greenock.

All *Now* photographs were taken by Bill Clark.

Online References

https://friendsofwemyssbaystation.co.uk/around-pg-retrieved
https://www.inverclydeheritage.network/port-glasgow
https://www.undiscoveredscotland.co.uk/portglasgow/portglasgow/index.html
http://www.geograph.org.uk/article/A-History-of-Port-Glasgow
https://en.wikipedia.org/wiki/Greenock_and_Ayrshire_Railway
http://thegreenockian.blogspot.com/2020/07/john-wesley-preached-here.html https://www.prefabmuseum.uk
https://www.poheritage.com/Upload/Mimsy/Media/factsheet/93980NORDIC-CLANSMAN-1974pdf.pdf
https://s3-eu-west-1.amazonaws.com/s3.spanglefish.com/s/38288/documents/john-s/port-glasgow-landed-gentry-and-gentleman-farmers.pdf

History/Origins

The town had been founded on a flat area of raised beach, extending back to a point where the land starts its steep rise, beyond where the railway line runs today. Today's town centre still retains the original form of the street grid, first laid out by the town planners from around 1693, where streets cross at right angles. Close inspection of the shape it formed suggests that this part of the shoreline was originally a promontory jutting out into the river at the edge of the raised beach, with Scarlow Street and Fore Street running along its edge.

Trade increased rapidly during the 17th century, with ships importing tobacco, sugar, rum and cotton from America, and timber, iron and hemp from the Baltic. Though well known for trade, and later for shipbuilding, it is a little known fact, however, that during this period the town was famous for its fruit. In the latter half of the 18th century, land was leased in plots as far west as Inchgreen for use as market gardens. The fruit was brought daily to the port for transport to Glasgow on the river steamers. However, sometime around 1833, the upper Clyde was deepened and the town became less important as a port, as ships could now sail directly to Glasgow. The first shipbuilding yard had been established near Newark Castle in 1780 and Port Glasgow was soon to become a centre for the industry, as this took over as the main source of employment and was eventually responsible for about a quarter of the total tonnage of ships launched on the Clyde. By the end of the 19th century, the waterfront between Newark Castle and Greenock to the west was occupied entirely by shipyards. Large timber-holding ponds were created along the riverbank to the east of the town to store imported timber intended for use in the shipyards. These ponds stretched from Newark Castle to Langbank, and evidence of them still exists today, as heavily weathered posts that once secured the logs in place, known locally as the "Stobs". Today, the shipbuilding industry has all but gone and only the Ferguson Marine yard remains.

Geology/Topography

Much of the coastal fringes of Inverclyde and North Ayrshire are what is described in geological terms as 'raised beach' – narrow areas of flat ground often backed by what were once sea cliffs. During the last Ice Age, Scotland was overlaid by a vast thickness of ice, the weight of which pushed the Earth's crust down into the mantle. When the ice melted and the pressure was relieved, Scotland began to rebound and the land lifted. Sea level fluctuated as the ice sheets grew and receded during the Ice Age, but eventually stabilised and the continued rising of the land, which is still ongoing, caused the shoreline to recede, leaving relatively flat areas that were once tidal margins, composed of sand and gravel. The towns of Port Glasgow, Greenock and Gourock were founded on this narrow coastal strip. The landform that we see today, however, has been further modified by human activity. Development of docks, harbours and shipbuilding yards required large areas of land to be reclaimed – "made ground" in construction language. In the vicinity of Port Glasgow, the shoreline of the estuary has been extended by depositing several metres of fill material on top of alluvial silt laid down by the River Clyde. Evidence of the former sea cliffs is visible as outcrops of sandstone bedrock at the station.

This view of the East Harbour, dating to 1930, has been taken from the East Quay, with the Mid Quay on the right, separating it from the West Harbour. On the left is the Town Building, which replaced the town's 17th century tollbooth. This was designed in the neoclassical style by Scottish architect David Hamilton (1768-1843) and was funded by public subscription. It was constructed on the dockside in 1815-16, but now stands some way back from the

shoreline, as the East Harbour and the adjacent Wet Dock were filled in, during the 1960s, to provide land for the town to be bypassed to the north by the A8, and to expand Coronation Park. The two storey building with its Doric columned portico features a 150 foot (46 metre) clock tower with a copper weather vane, which carries a six foot model of a fully-rigged sailing ship (see inset).

This view of the East Harbour, dating to 1905, looks towards the Town Building from the Mid Quay, which separated the East & West Harbours, and on the far left, the Bouverie tenements are just visible. The Town Building no longer serves as the Town Hall, and now houses the public library on its ground floor, following refurbishment and extension work that was completed in 1996. The shape of the street layout on old maps of the town suggests that Fore

Street was almost certainly originally built along the edge of the shoreline of the raised beach, where a promontory once jutted out into the river. Any trace of this has long disappeared and Fore Street now stands well back from the river. Where the buildings along the dockside once stood is now occupied by bus stances. Probably few people today realise that the public toilets and some of the bus stances were once under water!

The two harbours created in the 18th century were separated by the Mid Quay, the outer end of which is visible in this view of the West Harbour, dating from 1930. The view looks towards the West Quay, on which the Jubilee Bar, the Custom House and a row of warehouses stood. Today, only the warehouses survive – now Category C listed buildings. The view looks across the harbour entrance, towards the Leading Light, which still stands at the far corner of the Mirren's Shore quayside. There is a local folklore tale, probably apocryphal, that tells how the shore got its name. The story goes that Mirren, a young Covenanter girl, was sentenced to death by a tribunal, during the "Killing Time" in the late 17th century. She was tied to a stake

on the shore at low tide, to drown as the tide rose, but was rescued by her boyfriend, who rowed out under cover of darkness to save her. It makes a good story, but can't be confirmed historically. The West Harbour was filled in and redeveloped as Coronation Park in 1937, to mark the coronation of King George VI, and what were once the outer harbour quays now form the riverside esplanade, with some small industrial businesses occupying its western end. The rock-reinforced part of the waterfront visible in the foreground of the present-day image appears to lie roughly where the original harbour entrance was situated.

This view from 1912, looking along Fore Street from a point on the Mid Quay, shows the buildings on the West Quay. Floating in the harbour are lengths of imported timber. These were unloaded and chained together into rafts for towing to the timber ponds mentioned in the introduction, where the water seasoned and preserved them. By 1914, this practice had ended – rendered obsolete by the use of pre-cut timber and precision steel for shipbuilding. The commercial boom in shipping during the 17th century meant that customs arrangements were needed, so what was then the principal Clyde Custom House was built in 1710 on what became known as Customhouse Lane. However, a replacement building was built on the West Quay around 1754, which

was in turn re-built in 1821. This appears as the central building in the old image – a two-storey, five-bay building, with an ionic columned entrance and faced with finely dressed ashlar stone, designed by architect William Burn. Plans show that the building was 'L' shaped, but the extension to the rear is not visible from this angle. The Custom House on the West Quay was demolished in 1967 and the site is now occupied by the Auto-Tec garage. The present-day view shows that the Mid Quay was located roughly where the traffic lights at the main town entrance now stand.

The date of this picture of the buildings on the West Quay is unknown, but it has probably been taken sometime around 1930, or possibly a little earlier. The building in the centre was the Custom House, which was, in fact, the third version to be built in the town. The original in Customhouse Lane, which dated to 1710, was superseded in 1754 by a new building on the West Quay, which was in turn replaced in 1821. The building on the left was the Jubilee Bar, which stood at the corner of Scarlow Street and Fore Street. The picture has been taken from the outer quayside, looking west towards the mooring

points, and seems to show that at least part of the West Harbour was tidal, as the foreground area appears to be mudflat. Much change has taken place here – with the filling in of the harbour in 1937 and the rerouting of the A8 around 1980. The present-day view from the now solid ground of Coronation Park shows that the A8 carriageway runs through the location where the Jubilee Bar once stood and the Auto-Tec depot now roughly occupies the Custom House site.

This 1920s view looks east along Fore Street towards Dockhead Street, from where a Gourock-bound tram is emerging. The side of the Town Building is on the left and on the right is a construction site, where the red sandstone tenements that stand there today are in the process of being built. Through the gap are seen the tenements at the corner of John Wood Street, so these must pre-date those on Fore Street. At the time, this was the main thoroughfare

through the town and the bus is heading east towards Bay Street. The present-day view has been taken from near the bus stances. Buses still use this part of Fore Street, though instead of passing to the right of the Town Building they now turn off to the left and onto the bypass.

This view, looking up John Wood Street towards the station entrance from Dockhead Street, is undated but the absence of vehicles suggests it was taken sometime in the 1920s or 30s. The street is named after the builder of the *Comet*, the first passenger-carrying steamship in Europe, which was launched in 1812. It operated from Port Glasgow to the Broomielaw, then back down to Greenock, greatly reducing the journey time. In 1962, to commemorate the 150th anniversary of the event, a full-scale working replica was made. The wooden hull was built by Thomsons of Buckie, and its engine was fitted by apprentices at Lithgow's Kingston Yard. The new engine was constructed at the Kincaid engine works, using plans that were held by the Science Museum in London. It

was launched on 1st September and made a trip to Helensburgh and back, with passengers decked out in period costume. The replica was put on display but has been allowed to fall into disrepair and its remains still sit forlornly near the Shore Street car park. John Wood Street is one of the few streets where the red sandstone tenement buildings have survived. Such buildings were largely financed by Lithgow shipbuilders, at the start of the 20th century, replacing less than adequate housing. A present-day view shows that the buildings that once stood behind and above the station on Highholm Avenue have gone. This location is now the Park & Ride car park for the station. Also evident are changes to the station entrance.

This view, looking down John Wood Street towards the harbours, from a point near the railway station, probably dates to sometime in the 1920s or possibly earlier. Major harbour developments, which had led to the construction of the West Harbour, the East Harbour and the Wet Dock, had turned Port Glasgow into a bustling port, and Scotland's first dry dock was opened there in 1762. This was designed by James Watt – pre-dating his later fame for his work in the development of the steam engine. It was 265 feet (80.7m) in length and 70 feet (21.3m) in width, with gates that were 33 feet (10m) wide. It originally used a horse-driven pump, but this was replaced in 1834 by a Watt and Boulton steam-powered pump. After ownership was passed to the Harbour Trust

in 1871, the dock was lengthened to 325 feet (99m) and the entrance was widened to 45 feet (13.7m). Also known as the graving dock, it lay near the bottom of John Wood Street, on the aptly named Dockhead Street, and a steamer in the dock is visible in the old image. The dock was operated by James Lamont and Company from 1935, when it was taken over from Lithgow shipbuilders, but it no longer exists, as it was cut off from the river in 1966, when the last of the dockland was filled in and reclaimed to provide land for the town to be bypassed on its northern side by the A8. No evidence of it remains and its location is now occupied by the Health Centre car park.

The town's first railway station was opened at the foot of Barr's Brae in 1841, by the Glasgow, Paisley & Greenock Railway Company, which was taken over, in 1851, by the Caledonian Railway Company. The present-day station still occupies the original site. In 1865, the Greenock & Wemyss Bay Railway Company opened a new line from Port Glasgow to Wemyss Bay, which diverged from the earlier line at Chapelton. Both of these lines, which were electrified in 1967, are still in operation. The fashions being worn by the passengers in the old view of the station appear to date the image to sometime around the

beginning of the 20th century. The view from the bridge at the foot of Barrs Brae also shows the upper end of Princes Street and the present-day image shows the changes that have taken place there, in addition to those that have been made to the station. Today, Port Glasgow Station is the only one on the Inverclyde lines where every passenger service stops.

Though the inside of the station has been modified considerably, the main part of the original Victorian cast iron canopy survives. The outer part that once extended to the edge of the platform has, however, gone. This was possibly necessary to facilitate the installation of the infrastructure that was required when the lines were electrified in 1967. The Victorian image shows that an impressive clock once hung in the archway on the left of the picture. Today, all that survives are attachment points from where something once hung – possibly a successor clock to the original, as these have been relocated on the arch. Though not visible from this angle, the station interior was enhanced in 2016, when a mural showcasing Port Glasgow's past and present was unveiled in

the entrance walkway. The eye-catching artwork consists of 14 separate panels, which measure 56 feet in total length. The project was led by Greenock-based RIG Arts, and the paintings, which combine then and now aspects, were worked on by local artists Jim Strachan and Karen Patton Orr. They depict local features such as Ferguson's shipyard, the Glen Mill, Parklea, the Comet replica, the former Scott Lithgow yards and the 'Endeavour' sculpture at the town entrance – each accompanied by a description to explain the work.

From around 1693 town planners laid out a grid pattern of streets on a flat area of the raised beach extending back to the present-day railway line, beyond which the land rises steeply. Much of this grid, with the streets crossing at right angles, is still in evidence in today's town centre. Approximately square in shape, the grid consists of Princes Street, King Street and Fore Street, running roughly north-south, and Scarlow Street, Church Street and John Wood Street, running roughly east-west. A view dating to around 1960 shows the crossroads at the Church Street / King Street junction, which lies near the

centre of the original town grid. Church Street took its name from the church which is situated at the far end, off to the left of the image. This was originally known as St. Andrew's, but is now Port Glasgow New Parish Church, following its amalgamation in 2019 with St. Martin's. The present-day image shows that the vacant lot at the far corner has since been redeveloped as an Iceland store. The red sandstone tenement on the near corner, just visible on the right, still stands.

This image from around 1920 appears to show the top end of King Street, near the junction with John Wood Street, so the buildings near the centre are 9-11 King Street, the oldest surviving buildings in the town centre – now B Listed. No. 9 was built as a Masonic Hall (Cumberland Kilwinning 217) in 1746, and is the oldest purpose-built lodge in the world still in use. In 1768, the Burgh Council purchased the lower section of the building to become Port Glasgow's first school, and headmaster's house. Around this time, the adjacent building at No. 11 was built, which became the first Town Hall. The site is of historical interest, since in 1772, John Wesley, Anglican evangelist and founder of Methodism, preached at the Masons' Lodge. On Tuesday 21st April, after preaching in Greenock in the morning, he arrived to speak in Port Glasgow and wrote later in his journal, *"Many gay people were there, careless enough, but the greater*

part seemed to hear with understanding". He was back in Port Glasgow the next morning, and his journal records, "I preached once more in the Masons' Lodge, at Port-Glasgow. The house was crowded greatly; and I suppose all the gentry of the town were a part of the congregation. Resolving not to shoot over their heads, as I had done the day before, I spoke strongly of death and judgment, heaven and hell. This they seemed to comprehend and there was no more laughing among them or talking with each other, but all were quietly and deeply attentive". In 2015, the buildings were deemed unsafe, as the roof was in danger of collapse, but Inverclyde Council has funded work to restore the historic building and make it watertight. Plans are proposed to convert the premises into a community hub – Port Glasgow Heritage Centre, to be managed by the local Community Council. The Masonic Temple will remain and will continue to be used by Lodge 217.

This view is looking west along Scarlow Street, from the point where it turns the corner and becomes Fore Street. The tram dates the picture to no later than 1929, when the operating company decided not to renew the lease because of increasing losses. A tramway had opened as early as 1873 between Greenock and Gourock, operated on lease by Vale of Clyde Tramways. In 1894, this was taken over by Greenock and Port Glasgow Tramways, which had opened a Greenock to Port Glasgow service in 1889. Until 1901, the line, which ran for a little under 7½ miles, was operated using horse-drawn trams, but electric trams were introduced in 1901 on a gauge of 4ft 7¾in. The company livery was dark red and white and the original 1901 fleet was composed of 30

large, double-deck, open-top bogie cars, manufactured by Brush, with seating for 30 inside and 44 on top. Since the line was entirely on the level, highly powered motors were not required, so each car was driven by two motors of only 25 horsepower each. Up to 1916, a variety of double and single-deck trams was added to the fleet and the one shown appears to be of this slightly later type. Today, the view looking back towards St. John's Church shows no evidence of the tramway.

Princes Street, which leads up to the station entrance, lies on the western edge of the original town centre grid layout. Today, it may be regarded as the main shopping street in the town and a view from 1972, looking across Shore Street, shows some of the businesses that traded there at that time. The equivalent present-day view shows that, in the interim, most of these have changed names. One constant, however, is the Sutherland Bar which is visible

on the right of the old picture, but from this angle is now partly obscured by trees. It is affectionately known to the locals as "Sudgie's". Along with King Street and Church Street, Princes Street now forms part of the one-way system that was introduced in this original part of the town.

This old image was captioned as Chapel Lane, but the name won't be found on any modern street map, since at some point the name was officially changed to Huntly Terrace. Nevertheless, local residents almost always continued to refer to the street as Chapel Lane, since it ran from near the bottom end of Princes Street, along behind St. John's Catholic Church and up towards the railway. Today, the area looks nothing like it did in the 1920s image, which looks east towards Princes Street. Only with assistance from Tommy Rodger, who was actually born in this street, at No. 21, was it possible to gauge an

approximate alignment with the original image. Tommy's family moved out in 1960 and the housing was demolished soon after. The rubble produced was used when the East Harbour was filled in to make way for the A8 bypass to be built. The area was redeveloped, into the form we see today, in the 1970s. Tommy was happy to return there to describe the changes and pose for this photograph taken near where his birthplace once stood.

Many of the old pictures that still exist show alleys and closes among the original housing of Port Glasgow. However, most of these places are impossible to locate precisely, because so much has been cleared away after people had moved out to the new areas above the old town, where most of the population lives today and which has become known as Upper Port Glasgow. One exception to this, however, is Back Row Lane, shown in a 1920s image captioned

as having been photographed from Chapel Lane. The crane in the background confirms that the view has been taken looking north towards the river. Discussion with a local resident has determined that the location would have been near what is today the space at the junction of Shore Street and Princes Street, containing the raised flower beds. This is opposite the Sutherland Bar and is sometimes referred to by locals as "Sudgie's Gardens".

Once upon a time, Brown Street was part of the main thoroughfare and tramway that passed through the town. West to east, this was composed of Ardgowan Street, Belhaven Street, Brown Street, Shore Street, Scarlow Street, Fore Street, Dockhead Street and Bay Street, but all of these are now bypassed by the main stream of traffic. No continuous route along the original path is actually possible today, as Belhaven Street and Bay Street are no longer through routes.

Brown Street, however, still provides a back route from the Glen Roundabout into the town centre, running behind the retail park. The area has changed considerably, so the buildings at the Shore Street end are long gone and the area is now a car park. Where the viewpoint was for a view dating to 1903 was difficult to determine with certainty, so the present-day view may not be exact, but should serve to illustrate the changes that have taken place here.

The area known as "The Glen" was located on Ardgowan Street and is shown in a view dating to the start of the last century. The location took its name from the nearby Glen Mill, which manufactured sailcloth. A clue to the location is given by the slight curve of the tram lines, since old maps show that the line ran absolutely straight along Ardgowan Street and only made a slight deviation as it passed into Belhaven Street. This allows the approximate viewpoint to be identified for the present-day view, since absolutely nothing else remains that could have been used to precisely pinpoint the original location. The Wine Vaults and adjacent buildings are long gone, as are the tenement buildings and shops that once stood opposite, which were demolished in 1974, and

this once populated and bustling location is now a quiet backwater, with little traffic passing through and only the occasional pedestrian making their way down from Lilybank or heading home from the retail park. Visible in the present-day view is the viaduct, between the Glen and Kingston Roundabouts, which carries the A8 over Ardgowan Street, bypassing this part of the town. Beyond this fly-over lies Kingston Business Park and Industrial Estate, where things are a little busier. The area off to the right, beyond the storage tanks, was where the Glen Mill once stood and which today is occupied by a B&Q store.

The viewpoint for this original image, which dates to 1905, is at the eastern end of Lilybank Road, looking down to Glen Avenue. In fact, the image was wrongly captioned as "The Glen Bridge", since the bridge here is actually Chapelton Bridge. The Glen Bridge is lower down, where the Glen Burn runs under the Ardgowan Street / Belhaven Street junction. Major work was carried out at Chapelton Bridge in 2018/19 to widen the road and to strengthen the old bridge. Once upon a time it only needed to support horses and carts, but since this has now become a bus route, it required a major upgrade. The new road deck was formed using six 11-metre long pre-stressed concrete beams, each weighing 32 tonnes, which were dropped into place using a 300-tonne

capacity mobile crane. The project is estimated to have cost around £650,000. The consequence of this work was that Lilybank Road and Glen Avenue had to be closed for several months. On the left of the picture is the pathway that leads down to the railway bridge, which also crosses the Glen Burn. This path features in a painting by English artist, Sir Stanley Spencer, titled *The Glen*, dated 1952, which depicts children playing on the railings. Spencer had been commissioned as an official war artist during the Second World War, and travelled to Port Glasgow in 1940 to create artworks of the Lithgow shipyards, recording the contribution made to the war effort by Clyde shipbuilders. Post-war, he painted several scenes that depicted the town.

This view of the Scott Lithgow Kingston Yard dates to about 1973, shortly after the amalgamation of the Scott's yard in Greenock and the Lithgow's yard in Port Glasgow, which had become effective on 1st January 1970. At this time, there was a concept of building VLCC (very large crude carrier) tankers in two halves and joining these together after launching. The ship on the slipway appears to be the stern half of the *Naess Scotsman*, which was launched in April 1973. By the time the bow section was launched in January 1974, the ship had been renamed the *Nordic Clansman*. The completed tanker, which was

344 metres (1130 feet) in length, had a very short lifespan of less than ten years, as it was broken up in Taiwan in August 1983. Scott Lithgow ceased trading in 1993 and the Kingston Yard has all but disappeared, to be replaced by the retail park. The Goliath crane was brought down by explosives (at the second attempt!) in 1997, but close inspection of the present-day image will reveal that the ends of the piers that it once ran on are still discernible, as the very last vestiges of shipbuilding there.

The Chapelton area lies at the western side of the town, adjacent to the Lilybank area. This is close to the boundary with Greenock, so this view down-river shows areas of the latter rather than of Port Glasgow. Features clearly visible are the Titan crane at the James Watt Dock, the former Admiralty jetty at the Great Harbour and the Inchgreen gasworks. Chapelton is where the Wemyss Bay railway line deviates from the Gourock line. The line at the bottom-left is neither of these, but the Upper Greenock line that once ran from Glasgow St. Enoch to Princes Pier and no longer exists. Passenger services from Glasgow on the line survived until 1959, when they stopped running beyond Kilmacolm. Freight continued to be carried until 1965 and the line finally

closed in 1966. To enable the line to cross Devol Glen, south of Chapelton, the 'Nine Arches' viaduct had had to be constructed. Sadly, this impressive Victorian structure no longer exists as it was brought down using high explosives in 1970. Finding a modern equivalent view proved difficult, as the slopes to the west of Devol Glen are now covered by housing developments. The original higher elevation viewpoint is blocked, so the present-day image has been taken from a slightly lower point, which was only made possible by the existence of a small grassy 'window' area between houses. The angle is, however, close to that of the original, and shows the same landmarks.

Bay Street was once part of the main thoroughfare of the town. It lay at the eastern end of the tramway that ran from Gourock to Port Glasgow until 1929. The tram lines and an approaching tram are visible in a view from 1914, when the street was clearly busy and heavily populated, with tenement housing along its length. The view looks west towards John Wood Street, across the junctions with Victoria Street and George Street – short streets that once ran off to the left to connect with Station Road, which ran parallel to the railway. This area has been completely redeveloped and has changed utterly. The tenements have long disappeared and Victoria and George Streets no longer exist – with Court Road now occupying the approximate area where these once were.

Bay Street itself is no longer a through road, but is now split into two parts, with an area between where, in the 1970s, three tower blocks, Heather, Thistle and Rowan Courts, were built. These were renovated in 2010 and, unlike similar blocks elsewhere, many of which have already been demolished, they seem to have remained popular with the occupants. Two of these blocks are shown in the present-day view, which has been taken from a point that allows the surviving red tenements at the end of John Wood Street to be seen in the distance, so that the perspective approximates that of the original view.

This view of Blackstone Corner, where the Jamieson Restaurant stood, is undated but appears to date to the very early part of the 20th century. All this has been swept away and the area is unrecognisable today, but for the presence of the former Gourock Ropeworks building. Alignment with this allows the angle of the original picture to be determined. The Port Glasgow Rope & Duct Company had been founded in 1736 and merged in 1797 with the Gourock Ropework Company. This already had a worldwide reputation for the manufacture of ropes, canvas and sailcloth, and the growth of the shipbuilding industry on the Clyde was about to propel it to even greater prosperity. In 1814, the company was bought over by the Birkmyre family and, by 1887, trade had been multiplied by the addition of netting, twine and steel to the product range. The company was also famous for an important development when

it devised a way of weatherproofing fabric by chemical impregnation, producing a product known as 'Birkmyre's Cloth'. Following an amalgamation with New Lanark Mills in 1903, cloth manufacturing was transferred there. By 1954 the company had large operations both in the UK and overseas. In 1970, it was taken over by Bridon Fibres & Plastics, and operations in Port Glasgow were closed down in 1976. The surviving seven-storey red-brick edifice, dating from 1860, had formerly been a sugar refinery prior to being acquired by the Ropeworks in the 1880s. Conversion of the Category A listed building, which lay derelict for years, into 35 loft apartments, was completed in 2008.

The original church building, shown in a picture dating to 1918, was consecrated on 25th March 1857. The building was financed by a gift from the eldest daughter of a local laird, Sir Michael Shaw-Stewart, Jane Shaw-Stewart, a nurse who accompanied Florence Nightingale to the Crimea. She had inherited a considerable fortune from her mother and paid for the church, parsonage, a schoolhouse and a school-master's house to be built. It was a Scottish Episcopal Church, referred to locally as "The English Church", and stood near the riverbank at Clune Brae foot not far from Newark Castle. Under a compulsory purchase order issued in the late 1970s it was demolished to make way for the new A8. Conversations with local residents revealed that the

church once sat where the Newark Roundabout is located today. The exact orientation was uncertain, but alignment with the ridgeline behind and taking shadow direction into account, the present-day angle shown of the area must be close to that of the original. The church was replaced by a new St. Mary's of modern distinctive design, which is located at Bardrainney in upper Port Glasgow, adjacent to the Kilmacolm Road. Officially called 'The Church of Saint Mary the Virgin', the new church was opened in 1984 and incorporated many of the original furnishings and stained glass windows.

This image, which must date to around 1914, looks west along Springhill Road from the top of Bouverie Street. Firth View was the row of tenement housing, with shops at street level, on the left. Beyond there was a small gap, separating it from the original Springhill bow-window tenements further down the hill. On the right is part of the top end of the row of Bouverie tenements, which had been built in the mid to late 19th century and was claimed to be the longest continuous row of tenement housing in Europe. Its construction was the result of Port Glasgow's expansion, forced eastward and upward by the

increase in population, and was intended to provide housing for mill and yard workers. Now only the Springhill bow-window closes survive. The Firth View tenements were demolished early in 1973 and the Bouverie ones in 2014. Road realignment has also taken place, as housing has been developed higher up to the left of the present-day view, in the area known as Whitecroft. In the 1930s, when there were still open fields behind Firth View, some local excitement occurred when a light aircraft crashed there.

Carnegie Park Gardens, Port Glasgow.

In the 19th century, the land east of the town comprised six estates – three small coastal estates of about 25 acres, belonging to 'gentlemen farmers' engaged in market gardening or rope making, and three larger estates on the slopes further back from the river. These were owned by 'landed gentry' – rich men whose income came from large industrial enterprises or rents from the farms on the estates. Fruit growing had sprung up as a local industry from around 1767 and coastal estates were created because the flat land with many streams was ideal for market gardening. One of these coastal estates was Carnegie Park (the others being Fyfe Park and Nether Auchenleck), which was leased for market gardening and dairy produce. One of the early market gardeners at Carnegie Gardens was John Yeats. Later, in 1899, it was occupied by a gardener called Alex McLaren. This is a late occurrence of fruit growing as after

1841 the coastal estates were affected by the coming of the railway. Also, in 1858, a large part of Carnegie Park was lost to the town's need for a cemetery. The farmer, Mr. Wood, applied for an interdict to stop the development, but was overruled, and the application was granted for a new burying ground about a mile east of the town. By the end of the 19th century, the town needed to expand, sounding the death knell for the estates, as house building accelerated. In 1900, the row of tenements known as Carnegie Park Gardens was built along Glasgow Road. By 1937, after extension of the cemetery and construction of the council tenements of Kelburn Terrace, Carnegie Park estate had disappeared.

This image, showing the prefabs on Bridgend Avenue viewed from Boglestone Avenue, probably dates to sometime in the 1950s or 60s. Even before the Second World War had ended, temporary housing was being suggested as a solution to the shortage of construction workers and the destruction of housing by bombing. The 'Temporary Housing and Emergency Factory Made Homes' programme was established to research and develop ways to address the housing crisis caused by the war. The result was construction designs composed of prefabricated parts – the post-war 'prefab', which could be assembled and erected by semi-skilled and unskilled workers. These were mainly intended to re-house servicemen returning from the war or people made homeless by bombing, and 156,623 are recorded as having been erected all over Britain between 1945 and 1948. Post-war, however, successive housing acts allocated money for slum clearances, so in some instances prefabs were erected to re-house people living in overcrowded or unsanitary conditions. Prefabs were located on bomb sites or open spaces, and were scheduled to be dismantled and replaced after 10 to 15 years. Some lasted much longer, however, and are still standing in some places, but not those on Bridgend Avenue, which have been replaced by modern housing.